Archaeology

and other poems

Archaeology

and other poems

by

Louis Gallo

© 2019 Louis Gallo. All rights reserved.
This material may not be reproduced in any form, published,
reprinted, recorded, performed, broadcast,
rewritten or redistributed without
the explicit permission of Louis Gallo.
All such actions are strictly prohibited by law.

Cover design by Shay Culligan

ISBN: 978-1-950462-23-0

Kelsay Books Inc.

kelsaybooks.com

502 S 1040 E, A119
American Fork, Utah 84003

for my Muses—Cathy, Claire, and Madeleine

Acknowledgments

Poydras Review: "We're Alive!"

Litro Literary: "Girls to Women . . . "(published as "The Player")

The Lake (British): "Lost Biblical Verse"

The Orchards Poetry Journal: "Vision"

Belle Reve: "Illuminated Book"

North of Oxford, "Old Bones"

Pennsylvania Literary Journal: "Photographs"

Raving Dove: "The Night We Cut the Pineapple"

Offcourse Literary Journal: "Recollection of Love," "Last Kiss," "death is," "I Jumped the Gun but Missed the Boat," "Infinity"

Adanna: "Alexandra"

The Tampa Review: "Kroger"

Rosebud: "Easter Feast"

Poetry Quarterly: "Geese"

River Poets Journal: "The Hidden Life"

Arlington Literary Journal: "Nothing"

Pennsylvania Literary Journal: "View from Consciousness," "Hauntology"

Hamilton Stone: "Other people"

Penduline Pres: "Weeping Man"

Shades of Gray: "The Professor's Wife"

Contents

I. Overture/Underture

We're Alive!	13
Weeping Man	17

II. Minuets

Woodpecker	21
This Morning	22
L'appel du Vide	23
Vision	24
Last Kiss	25
The Garden	27
Occasioned by a Visit to Hollins	28
The Professor's Wife	29
Geese	30
Easter Feast	31
Musing	32
The Recollection of Love	33
Pompeii Before Vesuvius	35
Infinity	36
Why Won't You Talk?	37
Nothing	38
Illuminated Book	39
Buzz Saw	40
Christmas	41
Wet	42
My Dog Daisy and God	43
Archaeology	44
Original Sin	45
Lost Biblical Verse	46
Desire	47
Hauntology: Origin	48
Happy New Year 2017	49

Mourning Song	50
A Vision	51
Blood Moon	52
Gratitude	53
Wise	54
Other People	55

III. Sonatinas

Stepping Briefly Aside	59
Absolutes	61
Debt	63
Girls to Women, or, Reflections in the Game Room	65
Residual	67
I Jumped the Gun but Missed the Boat	68
Land Line	70
more from Crash: A Sequence of Variations	71
Piano	76
Remember Me	78
Schopenhauer's Dogs	80
The View from Consciousness	81
Old Bones	82
Vinegar	84
The Raw & The Cooked	85
The Hidden Life	86
Elsewhere	88
Memory	89
Alexandra	90
Kroger	92
The Night We Cut the Pineapple	94

IV. Dirges

The Lord of Misrule	99
Photographs	103
Death Is . . .	105

I.

Overture/Underture

We're Alive!

It takes me by surprise to find no one at all on the track
of the rec center at my usual time around ten-thirty when
usually I'm surrounded by dozens of walking wounded,
folks in varied stages of disarray and diminishment,
the Geezer Club, people walking or hobbling or even
jogging tenderly for their lives, to add a year or so,
to feel better, who knows why? But today there's nobody
and at first I feel elated, the whole place to myself!
I can break all the rules, I can trek in the opposite direction,
lie down and roll if I want, take baby steps, giant steps,
do the Mashed Potato, I can sing out in dissonant
 hallelujahs and belch and make chicken noises, I can
lie on the floor, anything, I can do anything—

. . . but I figure surely someone will show up any moment, the
traffic is usually constant, but no, no one arrives and I'm on my
third lap now, and I start feeling a bit creeped out, like that
movie when todo el mundo disappears except for this one guy
who resorts to making cardboard people to talk to, not that
I ever want to talk much with anybody, but hey, you like
to think there are others, even only one other, not just
your sorry, desolate self trudging the lonely road, no

Whitman procession, nobody home, and it's getting to me
big time around the fifth lap, and the place is still empty,
and my imagination takes a nosedive and I'm thinking maybe
everybody on earth has in fact vanished and it's just me now,
for, see, this has never happened before, never, not in decades,
not even janitors or the fat gimp Chuckie who handles the
basketball court down below, nada, nada

and so I figure they all got hit, some angel of death sweeping
through, but missing my envelope, some swift-acting virus or
finally the atomic conflagration we've all awaited
since Hiroshima and I know it's crazy . . .

but I now espy slight hairlines in the track itself, fuzzy tendrils
of antediluvian vegetation sprouting from the walls, though a
smack to my forehead clears up the horrendous visions, but still
no joggers or walkers and I'm reaching for the eleventh lap now,
and I'm worried about my wife and daughters, have they too
disappeared?

and my half-crippled old mother down in New Orleans, has
another Katrina swept through? and Greg down at University
BP and that nubile cashier at Wades, and Mr. Evil down
the street and Daisy and Peaches and Sweetie and Baby,
and even Banjo, the stupidest cat in the world, and my sister

and all the school children and the president and the fleeing
Icelanders, are they all just suddenly gone? and it's getting
to the point that I think

I have no choice but to break my stride, head for the stairwell
and do some snooping around outside, like Hume opening
the door to make sure the world still existed, look for passing
automobiles, birds in flight, the garbage men (because today
is Monday after all)

when at my back I hear the west wing door creak open,
and I spin on my toes and see this hunched old soul waddle
in, struggling with getting off her coat over by the racks,
and I rush hastily toward her and she sharply turns,
alarmed at my pace, and I throw my arms around her
crying, "Thank God, thank God you're alive, thank God
you're here and we're all still here, everything's ok
because you're here, do you understand, I must hug
you, please forgive me, I thought the world had ended,
everyone but me. . ."

and of course she thinks I'm crazy and maybe dangerous,
so I back off, beg pardon, beg pardon, I even do
the little Japanese prayer thing with my hands, and I
hasten toward the exit sign and, with one last breath,

cry back at her, "Oh thank you for being here, you
have saved the city, the state, the planet, maybe
the universe, thank you, thank you, thank you," and I
leap down the stairs with more energy than I've

summoned in about a year and want to rush outside
and exclaim to all I see that, yes, we're still here,
maybe not for long, you know how time flies,
but at this precious iota in spacetime, we're definitely,
finally alive!

Weeping Man

The other day, when passing through the lobby
of a swanky hotel, I veered into the bathroom,
a swirl of marble, art deco tiles and brass fixtures.
There I found a man weeping at the urinal.
He sweated profusely. The man was losing
moisture at an alarming rate. Dehydration,
I know the symptoms. Get to the pool fast,
I told him, took care of my business and left.
Later, in the pool, a shimmering surface
of bikinied apparitions on rubber floats,
I found the man still weeping. Such bounty,
I cried, and yet you weep on. I shot off
the high board and dove into the chlorine.
I watched the weeping man trudge
off to the locker room, dripping wet.
Some of us are just damp all the time,
I marveled to one of the oiled beauties
who swam to me like winged confection.
I thought of the man and couldn't go on.
I can't, I tried to explain to my sullen consort,
twitch ecstatic in an unhappy world.
The young woman splashed noisily away.

So I went in search of the leaking man
who had darkened my life. I would admonish him.
I sleuthed, found his room number, took
him by surprise. Except he wasn't in.
No suitcases, cloths, keys . . . nothing.
The room was sodden, saturated
with tears and who knows what secretions.
I shook powder into the carpet, sponged the walls.
To no avail. I have never seen the man again
but imagine him weeping on railroad tracks,
on the ledges of skyscrapers, in boiler rooms,
in some dingy automobile with a rubber hose
connected to the muffler. In outer space.
I pray to cut out his heart, that afflicted organ.
He cringes in the corners of my eyes,
lodges in my tear ducts, taunts me
me with liquid sadness. And now
I am not above a tear or two myself,
if only to wash him away.

II.

Minuets

Woodpecker

I spotted a small female downy
pecking at my front yard pine tree
this morning. She scampered up
and down the trunk, located a spot
and commenced the excavation.
I stood and watched for quite
a while because it seemed to me
the best thing that could happen
all day, observing that simple bird.

Bergson believed in two
kinds of smarts—the instincts
of animals and rational consciousness,
the latter both our privilege
and curse, the former a blessing
of ease and exactitude.

O, Mater Dolorosa,
when did your mind
break your heart?
When did your heart
break your mind?

This Morning

I stepped onto the porch to see
An owl perched in our willow tree.
I've heard the folklore of wisdom and death
But this fine bird augured no threat.
As for wisdom it had outwitted me,
Free as it perched in the weeping tree.
I stepped back and closed the door
To commence anew another chore
and deem that omen in hours hence
Exquisite and ample recompense
For living and dying the way we do—
Wingless and stalled while passing through.

L'appel du Vide

After the sprightly fifes and snares
You're off to war to thwart again
an invasion of raggedy-assed infidels.
But the commandant has gone mad
And you desert midway, heading back
to Annunciation where you drink rum
On the bank of a bayou and shoot craps
With the leftovers.

Or suppose it comes as the low throb
Of a bassoon tendriling its way through
The laced intricacy of Spanish moss
Dripping from boughs on a moonless night?
It ricochets in your skull, a meaty drone
Or wail of sad profundity signifying only
Itself and nothing you know or have known,
Its resonance freezing your blood and bones.
Or worse, when she looks you in the eye,
Kisses your lips and whispers," Follow me
Into the underworld. I will show you my grief
And it shall be your grief and that of the world."
Because you cannot escape from nor drown
In the bog of remorse subsuming you, remorse
For what you were given, now lost, the moments
Of splendor and joy and a tempestuous romance,
The music, the poetry, the rousing, radiant dance.

Vision

I sit by this fountain again and see
the years fluttering by like motes
as the bells chime and the sun sinks
behind a willow tree
and darkness spreads like frothy ash
though my eyes still see
my shadow teaching the girls to ride
their bikes along the path
and later Peaches and Daisy
steaming across the sward
to catch the plastic ring we toss
and long before I see my bride,
before the dogs were born,
before they died, her hair long,
lambent, her eyes glowing wide,
and another child I see
who soared away with the wind,
a petal from our apple tree,
and I watch my father,
nimbused and pale walk toward me
to whisper goodbye
and as the years congeal tonight
into a burning moon
I weep as I did when a child
praying to atone
for all a fountain showers down
in a single splash
as we rise and rising, drown.

Last Kiss

The crowds had to part that Mardi Gras day
when a man costumed at the Berlin Wall
lumbered up Bourbon toward Canal. We saw
this right outside Laffite's Blacksmith Shop.
He consumed practically the entire street
and swayed from left to right to keep balanced.
A troupe of male ballerinas wearing feathered
jockstraps, and that's all they wore, hooted
behind him, protesting their blockage of passage.

The streets were so packed we felt suffocated
and veered off into the Shop for relief
though it too bulged with bodies, everyone
festive and drunk, some old dude plunking
the piano and a crowd of retirees singing along
to Fats Domino's "I'm Walking to New Orleans."

But it wasn't Mardi Gras for us. We came here
to break up after a year of relentless passion,
so intense we both agreed it would kill us
to go on. We found a shiny, lacquered table
in one dark corner, ordered the vodka martinis,
five each, straight up with olives.

After so much time you don't need words.
We gazed into each other's eyes, yours emerald
mine more hazel and our eyes spoke defeat,
benedictions, one blink in unison, a Sousa
marching band, the next, Verdi's great dirge.
Something like this happens everywhere
all the time but abstractions mean nothing
until they incarnate into the daggers
you plunge into each other's hearts.

The gift had been too much, too extravagant,
too merciless. We had learned the blessing
of restraint, unwillingly, of course.
Eyes now closed, we leaned across the table
and lip to lip kissed goodbye. And, oh,
what a kiss it was, a kiss of remembrance
as well as forgetting, and that kiss assumed
a life of its own, burst through the roof
of Lafitte's, scorched the crowds outside,
zoomed into the atmosphere and exploded
in some other universe. When we opened
our eyes again we had both disappeared.

The Garden

I would like to think that when I die
my atoms will disperse not in a frenzied diaspora
of splintery Balkan states but an orderly exodus,
some flowing into the tribe of red birds that
swoop each morning from the snow-tipped pines,
some into the pines themselves, and the locust tree,
others into the row of forsythia and honeysuckle,
into the squirrels, the butterflies, the flaming
hibiscus, the squadron of tiger lilies, the modest
althea bushes and towering silver maple, into the
dragon flies and occasional faun and chocolate roses . . .
so that I may behold the garden as it beholds itself,
through no lenses but its own, without me, yet me.

Occasioned by a Visit to Hollins

I, also pilgrim, stood on the bank of Tinker Creek
While awaiting my daughters to make their rounds
About campus. We had seen two white cranes
Soar overhead, later two turtle doves in the gravel,
And Maddie spotted a bluebird perched on a maple branch.
Good omens, we rejoiced, prophetic pioneering.

The rational mind knows only boundaries, chance.
It forgets what lingers in the sky, the roses, the trees,
The water and blue-black soil, what royal auguries
Slip in through vision, hunch, and dream, what
Animals know and those crazed out of education—
everything is connected, intertwined, from worm
To hawk, rainbow to stream, shamanic fusion.

There is no chance despite what logicians say
Nor time despite the imminence of Doomsday.
Nor did our cat Sweetie die the next day
Though a sudden knock at the door brought lilies
In a laced glass vase from the veterinary staff.

I'm kissing the joys as they fly today
As I should have done throughout the foray
From Ur to Nineveh to Jericho
But could not because locked in the prison-house
Of chronology. Neither angel nor beast,
I've broken free! For this moment at least.

The Professor's Wife

A fisherman and his young son
found the body yesterday
tangled in rotten netting
and ganglial vines
face down in the dark green
New River. We in town
drink this river.
The father described her
as white and bloated
with wide-open eyes.
There is no report on the boy
but we can assume his youth
suddenly ended.
I often walk at twilight
not fifty yards from the site,
soothed by the brisk currents
or mirrored surface of still water.
Just now, late one night
when sleep eludes me,
I open a tap, fill my glass
and drink water that tastes alive.

Geese

The geese freeze as I pass,
eye me with suspicion.
Some waddle toward the water
in case I suddenly charge;
others remain fixed
as lawn statuary,
their lithe black necks
contorted into the u's
of faucet plumbing.
I nod and move on,
happy they are here
and I am here,
not like them surely
but close enough.
Soon I have jogged on,
hear them honk behind me,
serene, content,
until abruptly they soar
on frantic wings.
What has frightened them?
I don't look back,
have no wings.
Something is gaining on us.

Easter Feast

We gather at the wooden table, spread with Belgian hand-stitched lace, a lead crystal bowl full of wet grapes at the center, and we wait, we wait for grandmother to return from the kitchen, a crypt of rosemary, sweet basil, and garlic.

The screen door keeps out the butterflies but not the pungent wafts of confederate jasmine, which nudge us like soft fists. Kisses. We wait for grandmother and her salver of lost bread, the small green pitcher of La Cuite, the powdered sugar, and slivers of iced strawberries. As we have always gathered on this holy day. For grandmother.

And as we wait, we watch each other slowly, gently disappear into milky gauze, then mist, then light, we turn into light. We are the light, the life, the resurrection, the body, the flesh, the body, the edible flesh of our grandmother, who smiles, hobbles into the room with, surprise!

a platter of fried plantains, our favorite. She is time, she is creation. We tear into the fruit with our teeth, tiny tombstones embedded in our gums. Our Father, you have misled us. We visit her grave. We have never visited her grave. For she is levity, a butterfly, the soul, breath of the ages, pneuma, the egg. Shafts of sunlight break through the tall French shutters as we feast, bleaching us invisible.

Our grandmother arrives with a bowl of glazed caramel flan. "Wait till you taste it!" she gushes. We dig in, stuff ourselves and pray, fade again into light, the luminous cream flooding this eternal moment when we laugh and gossip and talk small above the clanks of pots and pans in the kitchen.

Musing

Sometimes you just dry up like a powdery
old tree stump, which if you kick, disintegrates.
I've done that, kicked, and it's like in the movies,
poof! and you think back to when the tree towered
above the then New World, all those rings,
dating back to Virginia Dare, and now, see,
a pile of sawdust nobody loves wants or can use
for anything except as tinder to a blaze.

And this is history too, which is mostly books,
and they were once the towering trees,
and we all know paper is fragile, perishable,
so our pasts, however strongly writ, will also disappear
and those who come later can only surmise
about fragments of mandibles buried in quicksand
or what those pages might have said
and who reads them and why.

The Recollection of Love

Say you're remembering her
at a specific time and place years later,
maybe the tryst in old Jamestown ruins
or that rose quartz beach in Destin,
and she's remembering you
at that exact time and place—
that is, you're both remembering
each other then but are now in
distant locations and of course
many years have transpired.
Say further your memories are exact—
you remember what she remembers
precisely as it occurred.

Are memories shared in some
transcendent Platonic vault
outside time and space
(a place perfumed with the attar
of pleasure and desire fulfilled)
or do the memories reside locally
in each of your separate psyches?

I would like to think that we tap
into that eternal treasure house
(which, alas, also preserves pain
in a separate block of resin),
that what she experienced then
and there and what you experienced
then and there. . . ah, that consummation
in the ruins, that kiss on the sand—
persevere beyond the flimsy self,
await reenactment, thrill themselves
without us in a rhapsody of joy.

But I know enough about the mechanics
of mind, the ephemeral hijinks of time,
the relativity of space, to understand
that once is once and only once,
that the you and the she back then
have evolved beyond yourselves
and the mirror shatters because
it cannot bear such disfigurement.

And I know that the pasture
of memory is a false thicket
and will not endure or will transmute
into the way you tell the story.

Pompeii Before Vesuvius

> *. . .and rum was Plato in our heads.*
> —Hart Crane

Before Sweetie P. the cat went blind
before Peaches was poisoned and Daisy stiffened
before Cain slew Abel and Alaric took Rome
before the babies grew up and moved to Siam
before the blimp exploded and the Hittites vanished

we danced and sang in the breezy pavilion
we dined on truffles glazed with rum and cream
sucked marrow from the bones of peacocks and larks
winked at the suzerain's finest concubine
grew young and old in the broth of time

as now we persist, mere echoes of
the music of the spheres, soft specks of
the Queen's ivory fingernails, floaters in
Castiglione's retinas, shadows at
the wizard's back...we who once beheld
the tree of ignorance, its perfumed globes,
and did not eat thereof and did not die.

Infinity

From time to time I visit that monkey who
given infinite time will type out the complete works
of Shakespeare on his Olivetti.
He looked pretty haggard on my last inspection.
"Problem, friend," I said, "is that time isn't infinite—
It blossoms with the Big Bang and will wither
at the Crunch. You'll never complete the task."

The monkey glanced at me, smiled sardonically.
"You don't get it," he mumbled, still typing—
I think he had produced a few lines from
Titus Andronicus—nothing from *Hamlet* yet.
"It's hypothetical. *If* I had infinite time or you
for that matter, everything will happen. No matter
that I don't. It's the trip that counts. It's an old
Greek rolling the stone up a hill. If he had infinite
time, he'd get there. And, of course, he also wouldn't.
You've missed the point and will only grasp it
given infinite time."

As I left the dusty, disarrayed loft (he still plunking
away), I thought I heard the keys pound out
"Enter Lavinia ravished." And I thought:
Yet Shakespeare did jot down the complete works
of Shakespeare, infinity or not. Fancy that.

Why Won't You Talk?

I won't repeat what I've never said
because we all know the effects
of echolalia, that ear burn, words
backfiring on themselves in a Babel
of resentment, unspoken syllables floating
like tiny dirigibles loaded with explosives—

which is why silence strangles intention,
why the said pales beside the unsaid,
why nothing bespeaks everything,
why mute wisdom subsumes eloquence,
why chatter spreads like confetti spread
across every autopsy.

Nothing

I chastise students when they tell me
They can't think of a thing to write about.
I tell them to write about anything—a meatball,
A shoestring, a pebble in the street—just
Make sure the beauty and/or power
Of the words themselves transcend
The subject matter, since the subject matter
Is always the same in the end: love and death.
Think of the shoestring as a small noose
Around your neck or the meatball as a brain.

But now I too cannot think of a thing
To write about, I've been tabula rasaed
Into the ideational void. So I'll write
About nothing (no thing), which, turns
Out to be potentially everything, literally,
According to both mystics and quantum physicists.
Nothing, it seems, swirls with wave functions
And spits out virtual particles that sometimes
Become actual particles that comprise
Your meatball or shoestring or that pebble
No longer in the street but in your throat.
Or perhaps embedded in the meatball
That is tied and held together with your
Shoestring. See what I mean?

Illuminated Book

Late in the night, I caught her reading
the book I was reading, an old leather tome
with gilded edges, the book I was reading
the night before.
She raised her eyes and smiled,
closed the book and passed it to me
and in the transfer, our fingers touched.
Her hair brushed against my hand
as she turned and sank into the divan,
dreamy-eyed and out of focus.
I opened that book as I stood
to where I'd left off, but the book had changed.
Her slender fingers and gaze upon its words
had changed the book, had changed the words,
the words now illuminated, enflamed.
I reread the passage from the night before
and sensed that I too, had changed.
The book became a kiss, an embrace,
its leather velvet, its word a song
which compelled me now to sing along
and as I sang, she opened her drowsy eyes
and touched the book again, and her touch
ignited the page I had settled on.
Reading would never be the same.
I bent to kiss her lips and stroke her hair,
her wheaty wavy hair, and shyly she smiled.
Wherever I'd loitered the night before
was not where I lingered now, breathing
her magic and by her presence beguiled.
Breathing will never be the same.

Buzz Saw

Time is a buzz saw ransacking the knotholes
Of this board I push into the blade, a plank
Made for walking that I have walked
For many a year, plunging into one
Or another of the seven bountiful seas.
Drowning itself is not so bad—it's the rebirth,
The return, its heft, and girth that daunts
As you find yourself again ensconced
In still another episode of recurrence.
Why I have beaten back ravens with
Brooms and sticks, pitchforks and spades
And knocked them senseless by the dozen
Though they too soon reemerge, dazed
But unperturbed. They swarm the mastheads,
Shriek like harpies, nip at and mangle the neck
Of an albatross perishing on the deck.
Which the greater omen and why?
Not long ago a white submarine arose
From dark depths to torpedo my flimsy craft,
Knocking me senseless into an uncharted ocean,
Sinking the vessel itself upon impact.
I woke on a different, mysterious map.
That crash taught me nothing, nothing worth knowing,
Aside from the vicissitudes of chance.
In your allotted speck of season, weep as you dance.

Christmas

An old man sleeps in one of the mall rockers
beside a blazing stone fireplace.
He dreams of another Christmas
when his grandfather slept in a rocker
besides the wood stove at home after supper
with the whole family gathered in a room
he remembers as if it still existed. Someone
plays "Joy to the World" on a piano
slightly of tune. His grandfather dreams
of the future: that he sleeps in a rocker
in a vast emporium with canned carols
piped through loudspeakers. At some point
neither knows which is which, who sleeps,
who dreams, who remembers what Christmas.

Wet

I like the way things glisten
When wet—bricks, the lawn, skin . . .
Glisten, what a pleasant word.
And it contains listen:
As if to say
Hear the rain speak.

My Dog Daisy and God

My dog Daisy cannot believe in god
since beasts, as we know, have no gift
for an abstract reason, which one must have
to sustain abstractions.

How ironic that abstract reason
convinces me that god cannot possibly exist,
that the Red Sea cannot possibly have parted
nor any virgin give birth to a mortal
yet the immortal son of the very god
whose existence reason denies.
And yet when I behold my dog Daisy,
who cannot believe in god,
I believe in God.

Archaeology

I went into my back yard with a sturdy spade
and began digging up my past. Each decade
I flung into a mounting pile of mud and ash
until I came upon the first ten. I now stood
in a six-foot hole but sank to my knees
and pried every single year with a lesser trowel.
They yielded easily save the third.
I could loosen only a few pebbles there
and then, solid stone. I lay down in that hole
and tried to crack it with the dynamite
of my mind—to no avail. The first years
proved impenetrable, an oblivion I could not
plunder so like the oblivion to come, I trust,
alive but unaware, that dubious blessing,
an uneaten plum.

Original Sin

When I decided to give up chop suey
For Lent, figured I might as well include
The rum bonbons and flan as well.
What's contrition without renunciation?
Too bad Belk was out of sackcloth my size
Though I've smeared the ashes of my parakeet
(Zeke, who passed in untimely fashion)
To curry favor with the Paraclete,
That lonesome, graceful dove of outer space.

But who is ever truly shriven or forgiven?
Look, Maw, I flunked the test for blessedness.
How can we scrub out every speck of grime
From the wind-swept, dusty blast of time?
Some call it a bargain, I, defeat.
I hoped for green stamps, got an I.O.U—
Statute of Limitations, one day.
Lookie here, hyenas in the barn,
Termites in the spine, spiders everywhere.
Impossible not to sin, so beware:
Go here, not there, fly the filthy shrine.

Lost Biblical Verse

And it came to pass in those days,
depending on where you were,
that absolutely nothing happened
and that nothing begat peace
and prosperity and more nothing
and nothing transpired forevermore
until it came to pass once again,
as everything always does,
that nothing grew bored and
heavy laden and slew itself
into something heinous
that begat & begat & begat . . .

Desire

I like Rene Girard's notion that desire
is mimetic, that is, we desire whatever
solely because some Else desires it first.
Surely this explains why I once craved
that MG convertible because my friend Tom
drove one or the cheerleader I longed for
because everyone else did. . .
but how then explain Original Desire,
say, that of Adam for Eve unless
God, who created her, desired her first?

Hauntology: Origin

I wish Derrida wrote more beautifully
because this idea, while wrong, is beautiful—
no tracing an origin without seeking
a further origin. Sounds like Gödel's Theorem
of systems always leaking into higher systems
or Aquinas panting after God in that endless
successions of greater Goods. Russian
stack boxes full of cupcakes.

Or maybe it's not wrong after all. Maybe
the origin is hic et nunc—Alpha
and omega fused in the present moment
which, once stated as the present, is past.
I like it. We all contain the Big Bang,
which is the Ur origin, right? unless
we ask what came before the Bang—
apparently, nothing, a void, phantom
fluctuations of virtual particles, one
of which corporealized. Which? Why?

Well, I'm haunted. Haunto, Hauntas,
Hauntat, Hauntamus, Hauntatis, Hauntant.
Freud said, "He who enquires about the meaning
of life is sick." Count me sick. I crave knowing . . .
Otherwise, we're hula hooping in quicksand
on borrowed time without life jackets.
Could be worse, could be the birds
in my backyard pecking at a seed bell,
not one tiny husk of an idea. Worse, eh?

Happy New Year 2017

for Jack

Down, down the archaeological rungs
of childhood, how could we have known
that the Ur level in which we roamed,
tossing shells across the unpaved street
of Columbus, romping on the pavement
with cousin Jack, both of us deaf
to the drone of a phantasmal future
that had already ensnared us both
in the bones of its abstract jaws,
down yet not down, already flung
forth with no foresight or insight,
jellied as if smeared in years to come,
blown haphazardly under the sun
like dust toward some tomb, thrown
out of a kingdom in disgrace prone
to all born to bear the lead suitcases
of illicit travel, travail blasted out
of youth and ignorance and that vault
of time before time when we did exalt
the thin moment, and heeded a clock
that never chimed.

Mourning Song

Some spend lifetimes
mourning themselves,
others, others—
either way
the short end of the stick
winds up in your clenched fist
as you squeeze between
those mourning
and those mourned.

Hell, you're trying to get
to Louisiana
for the Strawberry Fest
so you can bite into
that red flesh
and savor its juice
dripping down your chin.
Somebody's got to do it,
somebody's got to forget
about the cruelty
of time, space and
what's that other thing?

A Vision

As I strolled through the botanical gardens
listening to the intricate melodies
of Bruckner's Second Symphony
on my iPod, I spotted her face
peering through patches of space
between the leaves of the great-leafed magnolia
and I knew that face, that pre-Raphaelite,
melancholic smile, the otiose emerald eyes
glittering despite tears, the sadness
of our spectacular universe.

I knew the history of her grief,
even madness—for what is grief
if not a child of madness?—
I sought the comfort of desolation
amid the influx of crushing beauty,
the gardens, the music, the remembrance
of ecstasy, her passion, her impossible
desire and my own yearning,
our chronicle of zeal limited to motes
in a shaft of light as are all things.

Oh, mystery of brief radiance,
never dwindle me to understanding,
never open my eyes, never never
raze this instant of delusion.

Blood Moon

for Cathy

Right after she left for work
and before I had yet to leave the house
she called to exhort me to go outside
and gaze at the blood moon.
It's beautiful, she said.
Her enthusiasm and joy, her
excitement, her taking a moment
to notify me, her desire to share
a moment of beauty
so enraptured me that I sat afloat
in wonder and thanksgiving.
The call itself far exceeded
any moon in beauty or rarity.
I sat in wondrous rapture
for so long that when I finally
arose to exit and witness that moon
the sun's glare had already
extinguished it.
I had missed the blood moon.
I had not missed the blood moon.

Gratitude

I fear it has all been some grave blunder,
a bookkeeping error, mistaken identity—
the largesse, the cakes, and ale,
the girls, kisses, poetry, and wine,
the lagniappe and party favors

peacock meat for some Asiatic potentate,
suzerain, Xerxes or Genghis, splendor
in Luxor, filigreed mignon,
gold, frankincense, myrrh

but I? who grew up on oyster-shelled
Columbus Street of no magnificent lineage,
I? with no bearings beyond groping
for the distant oasis,
I?

Some might call it luck, some delusion,
some grand larceny—
the bounty and glut, philosopher's stone,
the Grail.

Wise

All the codgers
making such fuss
over their long
etiolated deaths
the ceremonies
and services
and grand words
as if to outdo
what unwise beasts
manage in private
with no fanfare
poetry or regret
beyond a last
wondrous gaze

Other People

For Jack realizes Jill concretely,
And we do not.
                    —William James

Perhaps we would all like to realize
Each other concretely
Or maybe realizing Jill concretely
Absorbs all of Jack's time and energy.
Nor do we realize Jack concretely
Even as at this moment
He stubs his toes against a plaster wall
And howls in pain.
It's not our pain after all;
We have enough of our own.
And Jill . . . she is in the kitchen
Concocting jambalaya.
Thus we meet them as abstractions,
Old photos in an album
Of ancestors with our blood,
Yes, but ghosts nevertheless.
The missed opportunities,
The still-born embryonic love,
The one who disappears
Around a corner,
The one you had your eye on.

III.

Sonatinas

Stepping Briefly Aside

I'm thinking about what I'm not thinking about,
A sweet reprieve, a tablespoon of treacle spread
Over the bitter herbs that dissolve like acid
Down the throat, ah, glutenous golden syrup
Even if only a transient balm. Don't read
My mind right now, maybe tomorrow,
Maybe another day when it ain't storming outside
Since storms outside tend to creep inside
Given all those holes in the skull. Call the roofer!
I need shingles (and I don't mean the disease—
Them evil chickenpox residues, lurking, lurking).

Who would have thought it would have come—wait,
So awkward . . . who could know that it would come,
(better) to this or that—or is there another place
To deposit pandemic grief and/or apprehension?
Always what we want to do vs. what we must, eh?
Small portions of the former, glaciers of the latter.
I don't hold anything against anybody aside
From everything against everybody. Chew the bitter,
That's what happens. More treacle! Now! And
Some Southern Comfort, like drinking clouds.

I alone am not come to tell ye what you already know
Because I assume, correctly, that you too have pushed
That boulder up the hill. And, no, we cannot imagine
Sisyphus happy, how possible? Camus winks his eye
And provokes us to think otherwise—oh, that melodious prose.
Still prose, though, and poetry transcends prose,
Even when some prose is poetry, and it gets
Very confusing, so best to ignore, forget, delete, redact (ha!)
Like those lackeys who obfuscate the truth to save skin.
I just saw a photo of a savage, unholy brute of a coward
Who shot a giraffe dead—and Robinson Jeffers' lines

About hawks come to mind (wait, I'm trying to dodge
The mind)—he preferred to shoot a man rather than a hawk.
Why shoot anything?

So, lady, what I'm trying to tell you is that there will be
Attacks, rejections, dismissals . . . but you gotta persevere,
Rev up that energy field, bracket out Descartes
as he bracketed Out everything except Descartes.
You ask: why bother?
Who knows? Instinct? Ambition? Elan vital? Whatever,
The rose blooms brightly when it blooms, and brightly
Must you bloom, because, because, the deep river runs on.
And thus I conclude my trek outside the muck of mind,
Dive into the lagoon—can't see a thing through
such bilge—
To begin again, where I ended before I began.

Absolutes

They consume me, but I can't manage to claw
My way out of this heap of trashy relatives,
The this rather than the that, the nuances and iotas,
The frayed edges and wayward loose threads.
I asked that King of Absolutes, Plato, to help me out
But he just handed me a chicken and winked.
I sought out the Shaman, that most fearsome
Antlered man, who said: "You must climb
Past the rungs and scale pure ether."
I did so only to fall fastback to earth into
A damp haystack where, as luck would have it,
I met my Lucy in this vast, obscure junkyard.

Hell, we just lie back in our rotten armchairs
And watch tv shows from the 1950s
On our old Philco cathode-ray set with rabbit ears;
We poke along with sticks and find forgotten
Or thrown-out treasures like the cinnabar necklace
Dangling from Lucy's neck—so what if it's missing
A few beads; or this diamond-studded Timex
Wrapped around my wrist—so what if it's lost
Its diamonds and doesn't tell time? Who needs time?
So many yummy delicacies in the garbage bins,
Hardly spoiled at all. And we ate Plato's chicken
Straight off. Even have a few hounds guarding us
At night when the moon hangs low like a lemon
And stars spell out our names in the infinite sky.

As for verticals, I've long since abjured them
As more worthless than the rubbish consigned to us.
And, Lucy, not a greedy bone in her body—she's all
Mercy and passion and heart. We'll get married
Some day for sure, but no rush when you're having
A good time. Oh, look, she's found an entire pizza

In one of the cans, pepperoni! Only one slice missing.
It will go good with the cache of ancient wine
I dug up from the days of Edgar Allan Poe.
Vinegar now, probably, but we like vinegar.
Amazing how great life can be when you give up
On it and suck the marrow out of the dregs of the past.

Debt

Down the block from our house on Columbus Street,
there stood on the corner the neighborhood grocery,
Grouse's, one side of a run-down shotgun with unpainted
rain-gray weatherboards, the other rented to an old woman
slouched in a wooden wheelchair who spat mouthfuls
of baking soda solvent into a galvanized vat at her shins . . .
such grocery stores no longer exist, of course,
the creaking wooden floors with holes here and there,
the petulant ceiling fans, the wooden shelves—
everything wooden!—except the porcelain case
with glass doors for frozen stuff, and there wasn't much
of that, and an ancient Coke machine with its bottles
aligned on metal racks—you had to slip
a nickel into its slot, something would clank
and then you slid out a half-frozen Coke.

This long before super-stores, before McDonald's,
7-11, Burger King and even Holiday Inns—
didn't think I could remember so far back, eh?
And we relied upon dim-witted, sallow Mr. Grouse
to keep us supplied with fresh French bread, catfish, shrimp
and all those cans of beans and anchovies and tomato paste,
the jars of Crystal preserves, mint jelly, loquat jam
and fresh vegetables, though Mr. Grouse's cat sometimes
lounged atop the broccoli and cauliflower
(its hair often winding up between our teeth)
and his skeletal, mangy hound liked to park
between the crackers and baking aisles . . .

But what I loved most was the candy display
upfront right under the brass art nouveau cash register,
sealed with glass so we kids couldn't lift the Milk Duds
or Bazooka bubble gum, and of that precious cargo
I loved Luden's cough drops best of all

because at the center, which you sucked madly to get at,
sizzled a speck of salt or something slightly bitter
(and Luden's remains the same to this day!)
which sort of neutralized that rush of red, joyous sweetness.

And thanks to Luden's I became a capitalist,
felt Adam's Smith's invisible finger nudge me onward
(at six years old!), and I remember the exact moment
because I didn't have the nickel but craved a box
and when Mr. Grouse pulled it out for me, I beamed,
"Charge it!" just as I'd heard my mother do . . .
and he tallied the sum in his mottled notebook
and I sauntered out of the store, proud, confident,
already in neck-high debt and therefore ruthless,
though as they say today, "empowered" . . .
Charge it! Charge it! Charge it!
And the Visas and Mastercards
would flow into my wallet swiftly
and I could and would
charge the entire world, as it has charged me.

Girls to Women, or, Reflections in the Game Room

This used to be a funhouse/
Now it's full of evil clowns.
—Pink

I drift into the shady joint, nothing else to do,
and watch a few sharks perfect their torque
on green felt. Not my game, though.
I'm partial to the pinballs, the older
and more wooden the better.
Most are dormant, asleep, ignored by the young punks
who opt for ivory or electronic games
of mayhem and massacre.
Yet two quarters will catapult these relics
into frenzy
after all these years and sweaty palms.
Little swatches of Las Vegas right here in Nowhere.

Lisa, stalked by identical twins who scream,
hiss, and brandish garden clippers,
swallows ten mg. of Ativan each day.
Uncle George molests his niece Casey
when on her fourth birthday he sets her on his lap.
The god Pan makes love to Rhonda, Rachel
and Ashley, who turn to lithium, Wellbutrin
Prozac, and kill sex with chemicals.
Vanessa smells dead babies in the earth.
Kathleen watches blood trickle
from her nostrils, eye sockets and ears.
Kelly describes her night sweats and tremors
as just punishments for a wicked life.
She has wrapped her breasts with barbed wire.
Luci has befriended Christ and can talk
of nothing else. Christ is an ice cube
in her non-caloric sweetened tea.

Suzy's lost twenty pounds. Her teeth
spin like the blades of a propeller.
Stephanie has been exorcized
by a voodoo priestess in New Orleans.

These reports, some whispered in the dark,
some broadcast over PA systems at rallies,
have little effect on our lives. We weep perhaps
and stagger through each new day like drunks.
We have problems of our own.
We have inherited the women, our mothers
daughters and lovers, and yearn to seal them
in capsules which not even a single microbe
much less bands of despoilers can puncture.
Yet safety too is abusive and cruel.
So we shrug and bear impotent witness

as the ball rambles where it may.
We flip madly, curse, pound the worn sides
of the machine, until, inevitably,
it slips through, thuds into a hole.
The lights and buzzers scream TILT.
We drift away, nod to a rare next player
who drops silver into the hungry slits.
Outside, in the glare of this lean street,
Eve leans against a light pole.
She is scandalously clad and stricken with flesh.
We want her, and we don't want her.

Residual

I'm sitting beside the Buck stove fire
As darkness floats in to saturate the room
Like a sweet elixir. I am not quite dozing
And tranquil for a change when the snow globe
Left on the mahogany Empire sideboard
Begins its gentle tinkle of "Joy to the World,"
A leftover present from Christmas.
I remember when the girls were here
And our dog Cinnamon liked to chew
My shoes as we both half-slumbered
In this spot, the rarest room of the house.

That sideboard was constructed before
The Civil War; everyone was home for Christmas
Getting on now two months ago.
I am perplexed by the vast gulfs of time . . .
To think, some craftsman fashioned it
Before Lincoln, over a century ago, that
A snow globe makes music atop it,
That everyone now has gone back home
and I am here alone at the moment, remembering
How together we cherished the small good things
The world has to offer how we hated
Any disruptions, any changes that might
Beset us with shadowy dread.

As the flames lick their glass enclosure,
As the snow globe rains down snow,
As darkness, now velvet, cushions this
Armisticed mind, it is time not to move on
But to remain, to settle in, and rewind
The clocks until the clocks go blind.

I Jumped the Gun but Missed the Boat

Because I wanted to see the Kabbalist man of light,
Adam Kadmon, on display at MOMA, figuring
I might pick up some wattage myself in the viewing
Given this participatory universe. But Adam had gone dim
And I drove all the way from Baja for nothing, even
Got there early when the yellow cabs had not yet
Swamped the streets of New Amsterdam.

It's a problem, always early when everyone else
Always arrives late—and sometimes I remember
Nefertiti, her veils and swirls and attar, always
At a distance, because I missed the ferry to Cairo.
Nevertheless, distance lends enchantment to the view.
Who said that? It's not true. You want to gaze
Up close, the very pores, the eyelashes doused
With charcoal or ochre, the cracks of the lip.

Then onward or backward to the Gardens of Babylon
Where I trysted with Nausicaa—oh, not the princess
Smitten with Odysseus, but that sleek librarian
With tortoise-rimmed glasses and honey breath.
The gardens her library, the flowers, her books—
Imagine the arpeggios of passion and thus:

I met Brahms too as he strolled the promenade
With Clara Schumann, he much younger,
She renowned throughout Europe as Robert languished
In an insane asylum, crying, "Music killed me!"
He whispered to me, "I am dying to live."

I retreated hastily to Saskatoon, Saskatchewan,
Where the only thing going on was a renegade moose
Running amok through the streets, obliterating
Storefront windows with his antlers.

Oh, the perils and pleasures of everyplace,
The hidden nuances of geography, the latitude
Of longitude, the present tense of history!
I jumped the gun but missed the boat, though
Sometimes I jumped the gun because I missed the boat
And sometimes I missed the boat because . . .
Born too late, born too early,
Either way, there's poison in the gravy
And gravy in the poison.

Land Line

We still have a landline
Because so many old connections are still
Tied to it. Even came with a message machine.
Only occasionally do I listen to the messages
Because most are spam. But last night
I decided to clear and delete them.
Yep, twelve messages in a row—

And we're on the national DO NOT CALL
NOTIFICATION list!

The twelfth was not spam, however:
"Hello, it's Riverside vets. Just wanted
To let you know that Sweetie's ashes are here
And you can pick them up."
Expected, but I was still taken aback.
Our little kitty of fifteen years had been
Incinerated.
It takes so long for the residue of death
To die.

more from Crash: A Sequence of Variations

I. Reminders

She tells me that she has photos
of the mangled Rogue, but I refuse
to look at them. I see that popular
vehicle on the road all the time,
the same color too, and my heart
palpitates. I knew all along,
somehow, that that SUV was doomed—
knew it in my then unbroken bones.
Of course, I don't remember the crash
or anything much of the hospital,
doped up as I was for pain.
I don't ever remember much pain
though I suspect a lot of it.
Sometimes I feel a full-body rush
of not exactly memory but what
might pass as memory: a sudden,
a brief sensation that I was mauled
by some monstrous force—
I pant for a while
before sitting on our sofa next
to the fire, think of the kindness
of friends, and fullness of being
washes over me like grace.
To have been obliterated,
to have returned, to hold her hand . . .
the remarkable twists of nostalgia
and delicious forgetting.

II. Sling

for Eric

Eric came over the other night
and we all ordered from Fu Lin.
He asked me if I remembered
his visiting me several times
in the Trauma Ward.
I shook my head, no, sorry,
I don't remember, but thanks.
Then he laughed, you had a time
with that sling.
Sling? What sling?
Another laugh, the one wrapped
around your upper arm and shoulder,
you know, for the fracture.
Then it came back, the black sling
that was so uncomfortable
I must have cursed a lot.
I guess I wore it for about a week
then joyously trashed it in the can
along with rotten, deliquesced
bananas and cantaloupe seeds.
Funny how shreds of memory
return when prompted.
Someday I hope to resurrect
the entire history of the universe.
Then we'll really devour
some Chinese, man.
Just remember you can't eat
the nuts. Who can? It's all
a matter of diminuendo.

III. Prison Cell

> *Stone walls do not a prison make*
> —Richard Lovelace

You can feel the heft of the stone in those
Spondees and trochees, but that's immaterial here.
It was our tradition when returning,
after a long drive to New Orleans or Myrtle Beach,
to siphon Queen from the iPod into the car
radio speakers and listen to "Somebody to Love,"
waiting excitedly for Freddie to howl
"I just gotta get out of this prison cell"—after that
I would crank the volume to max and we all
joined in and howled along—
Oh, how we awaited that moment, all of us,
that brief moment of delirious abandon

and then the car crashed, and I felt the urgency
to listen to the road instead, to the mania
of other drivers, to pay full attention to the rush
of trucks smelting our bumpers, that is,
to remain in the prison cell of silence, of
apprehension, of fear . . .

and yet, and yet, almost two years later,
returning from Winston Salem, I took the chance
again. And, screaming, we broke out!

IV. As A Watchman Stood

But the owl was blind.
She tells me that immediately after
the crash groups of first responders,
ordinary people who happened to be
at the crossroads, rushed over to help.
She tells me I was conscious and walked
out of the wrecked Rogue and chatted
with the ambulance medics, hoisted
myself up onto the gurney.
I remember nothing of it, nada.
I awoke in the ambulance to call
my daughter, three times I'm told.
Then out cold. I don't remember.
Remember nothing about the Galax place
where they administered x-rays galore
and who knows what other tests.
Remember nothing about the transfer
into another ambulance on a rainy drive
to Wake Forest Baptist. Remember
nothing about being wheeled into Trauma.
Yet I'm told I chatted with all the medical
personnel on hand, even laughed a bit.
Remember no pain whatever—highly
doped up I'm told and would remain so
for two months.

I wanted to believe that I was talking
in my sleep, somnambulating as well.
I wanted to declare that if something
is not remembered, it didn't happen.

I wanted to believe that consciousness
is tantamount to clarity, even vision.
Then I did remember everything I've
forgotten throughout life, everything
that really happened (allegedly) but
has disappeared through the wormholes
of mind. Where do they re-emerge?
Does someone else remember (yes,
in the crash case, but what about the
rest of it?) What happens when no one
remembers? What becomes of us?
What of wisdom, experience, joy, despair . . .
what of the merest tidbits of the carnival?
The lovers and great poems? The children?
That sound and fury line comes to mind.
I'll never forget that. Of course, I will.
And so will you. The owl is always blind.

Piano

At one time I could identify any note,
Without looking, that you played on our family Spinet
Propped against the stuccoed wall in the front room
Of our house on Columbus Street.
God, that was so long ago, and I've since
Lost the gift of perfect pitch—now every note
Sounds like C major except the sharps and flats.
But it had to be pressed on the ivories
Of that Spinet, the one on which Dad played
Mazurkas and polonaises by Chopin.
I listened raptly, tried to play them myself,
But reading music irritated and frustrated me.
So I figured out how to play certain melodies
By ear, my favorite Strauss's *Der Rosenkavalier,*
The glorious parts, grandiose waltz or circus music
You might expect from a carousel.

Just recently I sat down on our back-room bench
And thought I'd try the Strauss again
On the electric piano we bought some years ago
On which the girls could practice their lessons.
I hadn't touched a keyboard in years
But assumed I could still muster some finger magic.
Why not, why should we lose whatever meager talents
We have solely because time bludgeons us all?
I still knew where to put my fingers, still knew
The tune, the notes, how they followed one another
In strict succession, could still hear it inside my skull.
Surely, I could still manage at least a slower version.
But no, my fingers needed oil, some elixir,
Some of Ponce de Leon's miracle water
To loosen them, to massage them into instruments

That coaxed out beauty. Too late, could not
Remember even Chopin's most dolorous,
Mournful slow preludes. What I did manage
Was a defeated and otiose Taps: CCF, CFA,
CFA, CFA . . .music, nevertheless . . . hey, Dad,

I can still play, not like you, not even like myself
Back then. As you used to preach—practice
Makes perfect. The bad news is that it's not practice
Or rather its lack, it's the years, their frets
and scores and tacits.
I had to dump that Spinet after I'd lugged it
From state to state for decades. It fell apart,
Lost its fortissimo and coda. But I think I lost more.

Remember Me

The strain of remembering what not
to forget, if not quite a muscular ache,
proves quite a heavy load nevertheless.
If wisdom is knowing what to overlook
I have become very wise by way
of stupidity. . . why once I could recite
the names of every Roman Emperor
from the first Romulus to the last,
the unperioded periodic table with even
its newly invented elements, the capitols
of every country in the world, current
or extinct—ah, Byzantium and Persepolis.

But what matter? What is cesium? Radon . . .
though the first can get you out of Dodge
before you arrive in Dodge, and the latter,
well, can kill you, the family, the dog, and cat.
Oh, and the lovely conjugations: amo, amas,
amat, amamus, amantis, amant (is that right,
I forgot?) Big toe, big totas, big totat—'swounds,
the totality of the totemic totalitarianism
of facts, of knowledge, of whatever you don't
need to know aside from SOS, Help! Run
for your life, Food, Wah-Wah, Quiero Dinero.

I would put on my white sombrero, Abba,
but I lost it down in the Yucatan when
Gila monsters invaded by land, newts by sea.
Oh-o say can you see. The dawn's oily light
never seemed so far away as on this expedition
west, Ulysses, gone a long time.
And what if nothing matters? Is that indeed

not the case, the case being everything
that is not the case? Given, I mean, that forecast
you read about in *Heat Death of the Universe*.
Sometimes it's just a matter, as old Dad said,
of rolling with the punches, though, if so,
who thought up inertia? Gravity ascendant,
levity sinking. But don't worry, I'll never
forget your eyes, honey, the ones that see
through mine, the ones that shine like sheen
in this otherwise opaque sea of dreams.

Schopenhauer's Dogs

I've had it with false premises, the confectionary
wishbones of philosophers and holy men who tender lies,
I'm fed up, for now at any rate, because I have witnessed
abominations of body and spirit, some first hand, that
discordant xylophone of cracked ribs, others not,
the perpetual victims of crime, catastrophe, evil . . .
and nothing can atone, however many Happy Faces
we wear, however many "Have a Nice Day's" we endure
from strangers behind glass windows who receive
our money, who pass a bag of fried muck into our hands,
Have a Nice Day, they chirp on command and pocket
minimum wage and never make ends meet, yet party
at Houlihan's every night and maybe OD on tainted
crack when they get home because what is life
but the release of crack, while the oligarchs
dine under crystal chandeliers with gold utensils.

I'm fed up, I say, and rightly so, though it will pass,
I pray, especially if I conjure up my dog Cinnamon,
and those before, noble Daisy and that clown Peaches,
all three of whom I'd set against the entire tableau
of both the apologists and the wrecking ballers, that woe,
as more sanctified, naturally, and moral and wise,
not a mise en scene I could have devised, just a lesson
I learned from my dogs, beasts, you hear, beasts
according to the record, and we, neither angels
nor beasts, too bad, too bad, not to be beasts,
the angels too busy strumming their harps to care
about who got splattered or when or where.

The View from Consciousness

When I first encountered Freud's notion
that "consciousness is a disease"
I sat between two venerable magnolia trees
as sultry coeds ambled lazily by, at ease
with themselves and my roving eye.
I was young and on the prowl, and to be
so disposed of required, I supposed, precisely
what Freud dismissed. Hence, in similar fashion
I dismissed the idea as rank (pun intended, Otto)
nonsense and opted for a plate of red beans,
rice, and andouille at the Underground Cafe.
As years passed and memories, both sour
and sweet, accrued, it seemed the deficits,
not the interest, not the whipped cream
and bonbons, accumulated more fiercely.
Therefore I sat me beneath a yew in mid-winter
(the magnolias had long since shed themselves)
and re-thought thought. Two mourning doves cooed
from an upper bough, a squirrel darted by
with a plump acorn in its mouth. I rued
the evanescence of days, the brutal magnetic tug
forward into time's moist jaws—and the coeds
had vanished into hovels or mansions elsewhere.
I savored the coo, regarded the squirrel
and the primal bark into which my back had fused.
And understood. And agreed. More than agreed.
One need not grasp the acorn to grasp it.

Old Bones

When I swivel my neck now, I hear
cartilage popping and although it feels good
I think instantly of old Hasdrubal of Carthage
leading elephants across mountains
and I think of the bones in our back yard
on Columbus Street that my dog Spottie
buried, dug up, buried again, sucking
out their sweet marrow, and I think too
of the catacombs in Mexico City
that terrified me as a child—and
they still, terrify me—and of course, who could
not think of Ozymandias . . .
oh I think lots of things because
how intimate is ossification and better
gather the memories while you can
before the neck becomes less a conduit
and more a fossil, not grainy like Lot's wife
but solid, I like to think, marble,
a work of art some sculptor might carve
into a skylark or turtle or tiny peacock
that winds up on the family mantle.

At the moment I stare at the meat
placed before me in the Ancient Steak House
and can't help poking at the bone
with my fork musing that it might emit
a signal of sorts explaining the difference
between its situation now and before when it
lived inside a cow. . . and I think of angels
and ghosts and sprites and how one
might thrive without the bones
always left behind, eroding into dust

eventually, the skull and teeth and
fingernails and ribs and elbows,
the structure collapsed, the thinking
over, the old bones, old bones.

Vinegar

The effervescence of our days does not
proceed sprightly as do the oxygen bubbles
in a newly poured glass of champagne.
What we shed, skin, cells, hair, bone,
plods along year after year, for decades,
until finally, the wine turns flat and dull
and inert, undrinkable...vinegar.

Which may explain why that girl
once snapped, "You've turned to vinegar
on me." I told her that vinegar had
its virtues—cleans windows, unclogs drains,
droplets on otherwise boring salads
adds a little zest. Decomposition,
yes, but not utterly defunct—
think the Titanic's wine bottles.

Or venerability, though who would not
prefer champagne? Hate the stuff
myself—sickeningly sweet, bogus vino,
time for wedding receptions with
Lawrence Welk & Guy Lombardo.

Oh but you should have seen her,
vine ripe, lambent, her mind a torpedo,
the kind of woman you know
will change the vectors on you,
phase shift you into apple cider—
on its way, tart . . . heartburn.

If there's anything decent about aging
I have yet to discover it
and suspect vinegar's the good part.

The Raw & The Cooked

That cooked goose changed us, verging
on angels now thanks to the meat,
beasts of old no longer when we sucked its sweet
marrow—odd, don't you think? That barbeque
could lift us thus (as we *do* think), out of the sty,
glancing heavenward at the sky, an eyeblink
ago we lay with swine, barked with dogs,
even ate each other (we taste like fowl),
out of primal bogs, we soared as brain
shot forth tendrils and neo-cortex swelled
with ideas, music, dance, equations, and art,
a hard-fought journey out of beast—we pause,
pressed close to her loving breast one night
in June, crepuscular, airy, and the moon
bloated with neon milk, her peignoir of silk,
as we invented love, not the mere brute sex
of shadowy animals, we espy, even docile doves
in the eaves, and, ugg, grub worms in the blackened
leaves fecundating themselves, ugg ugg, out of slime
we emerge, hesitate, glance backward for a speck
of time, reminded that once we reveled in raw,
not a thought in our vacant heads and saw what
we no longer see except in flimsy remembrance
of ourselves purely savoring, not why, not but,
not where not when, not who—just hairy, brutish us,
content there, satiated, unaware.

The Hidden Life

In 1959 Sylvia Plath dreamed
that Marilyn Monroe manicured her nails,
Marilyn, though still alive, itched
to swallow those pills three years later;
and soon thereafter Plath's pruned fingers
turned a greasy knob until it hissed.
Me, I'm stuck with Mick Jagger.
He drifted forth in tattered clothing, meek,
spectral, not the raw Liverpudlian bloke on stage.
I'm here to help, mate, he said sadly,
fusing his rheumy otiose eyes into mine.
What you don't know hurts the most, he said.
Think I want this job? It's a hot little Swedish model
I'm after...but here I am, by the grace of St. Jude.
So if you don't mind, let's get on with it.

And that's it, I swear...he receded
into some cloudy vista, and I, heart-pounding,
shot up in bed. I just met Mick Jagger!
I cried at the darkness,
only to fall back into a deeper slumber,
remembering nothing the next morning.

                    So I relate this nugget
from the perspective of the dream and all that happens
beyond ourselves, the way autonomic nerves
sizzle and bristle without our consent or awareness.
All that churning, all that rock & roll.

Of course, it's a bit odd—
Marilyn, a woman, comes to Sylvia; Mick, a man, to me.
Should have been the other way around, should have been sexy.
Mick and I can still kick around some.

And suppose Plath dreams about Marilyn *now*.
Or Marilyn, Plath? Or Mick, me—
fat chance on the latter, but mysteries abound.
Don't you get this feeling that the pieces
of our puzzles have fallen into disarray?
Don't you just want God to arrive
with a corps of angelic engineers and cleaning people?
Bob Vila would do, maybe Miss Manners. . .
or some ancient Greek shoulders carved of stone.
It's what you get when wish fulfills itself:
niches, wormholes, cracks, and rips—
where real-life hides, where you hide, where Marilyn,
Mick and Sylvia hide, where secrets burst
into flavors so new, so startling, the universe changes.

The plot thins; you're back on the narrow,
waiting for some clink, chirp or *pssst* to happen.
Or not happen.Until again,
with the precision of radioactivity,
dream fangs puncture the jugular
and transport you drop by viscous drop:
an Atlas truck loaded with Marilyn's furniture
runs out of gas on the interstate;
Plath's casket of lost journals rests on a glacier;
Mick's larynx squeaks, a smudge of ash.
Me, I cling like a hangnail to the static
of applause that anoints with slow rain.
Me, I'm beating time on some dashboard.

Elsewhere

Metaphysics has nothing to do
with reality yet I am drawn to it
as a dog might respond to a distant
screech in the night.

Because I happen to believe
in what's not there
though where does it get you?
Relief? Hope? A swig
of ale brewed by Spinoza?

When Longinus went to work
for Xenobia, the wondrously beautiful
queen of Palmyra, had he already
constructed the Sublime?
Or was the Sublime an abstract
diversion from the beauty
of an untouchable queen?

Here's a sweet-tart from Palmyra.
Forget the demons and angels
swarming about the room
as you savor its nougat.
Your dog does hear something
though as he gnaws the juicy rib
you tossed from the table.
Brother, cur, beware,
of what lies elsewhere.

Memory

I stood in the aisle of a bookstore,
I stood there a while trying
to remember your name
though I well knew the title of your book
that had often transported me
many a night when its words
blazed brightly in the dark.
I sought another such book and fought
to retrieve your name from whatever
pothole of mind it had slipped into.
Thus I find myself, not often
but often enough, when in a store,
grocery or mall, coaxing the name
of a product, a person or song
to spring from its neural tomb
and wonder hard if this signifies
something unwise or wise.
We are told that forgetting
is the secret of memory
so useless data won't deluge
the brain . . .

But I remember remembering,
when I forgot nothing and functioned
beautifully in a glorious glut
of tidings—a young nation it was,
ah, a song, a movie, a poet, a poem,
instantaneous. Nevertheless,
I stood in that aisle, I stood trying
and once it came, I felt still blessed,
for it did come, it came, I had to wait
a while, old skull, and a bit late,
but you came, and I found that book.

Alexandra

In this noir photo, you look
like a besieged Catherine Deneuve,
besieged by furies, by fate, by demons,
besieged and defeated, yet for all that

hopelessly beautiful, a flower in the ruins.
And I imagine Marcello Mastroianni lurking
in the background of *La Dolce Vita*, winking

at Fellini behind the camera, yet desperate
to save you from evil, from himself, from Fellini,
from the world, from yourself.
And I see Max von Sydow in *The Virgin Spring*
avenging his young daughter's rape and murder
with an ax.
Catherine again going slowly mad
in *Repulsion*.
I see Truffaut, Jean Moreau's suicide
after losing Jim as (the great) Oskar Werner (Jules)
grieves over the extinction of his lovers.
I see Julie Christie and Dirk Bogarde
In *Darling*, his revenge complete.
I see Anthony Quinn and Alan Bates
watch on with horror as the villagers
stone the graven widow to death.
I hear Tony Perkins howling to Bach
while driving his car off a cliff
after sleeping with his father's new wife.
I watch Vittorio De Sica's
The Garden of the Finzi-Continis
And weep at the barbarous ruin of beauty.
You are a foreign film of the 1960s in one frame,
the kind I watched years later at the Peacock Art Theater
on Clematis Street, the Gentilly Theater
on the Chef Menteur, the Pyrytania uptown
in New Orleans or at film festivals in South Carolina
and Virginia—and now, alas, on YouTube.
One frame, one frame says it all: you.

Kroger

The twenty-four-hour supermarket gushes
fluorescence bulges with pomegranates,
loquats and sacks of pineapples from Honolulu.
Oh, pineapple, lush, juicy-entrailed gargoyle,
how Buddhistic you seem, so serene and lonely!
And who is that scruffy-bearded man dressed
like Uncle Sam hovering over the zucchinis?
Should we not alert the manager at once?
Entire boulevards of tins! Alphabetic pasta,
what great poem does the insidious can opener
destroy? Silly anchovies coiled like vipers;
young mothers in shorts pushing their carts;
slim bottles of capers with their rascally smell;
the chests of turkeys and chickens frozen solid;
neon popsicles; ziggurats of lethal chocolate;
old women munching on their own lips;
marshmallow whipped into a foam; bins of
voyeuristic pistachios; jugs of aqua from the Yukon!

Our baskets brim, runneth over, wobble up the conveyor
to Amy, dew-dropped cashier, lips pink as cream soda,
lustrous Noxemaed cheekbones, eyes the glow of kiwi.
Amy, Amy, can we purchase you as well?
You scold Doyle, the teenaged bagger, so deftly
when he ogles you, sag-faced Doyle, whose tongue
hangs too low, a mushy plantain bubbling
with the confectioner sugar of drool,
whose mind has never wholly formed.
But he loves you, Amy, as we love you, as the pineapples
and anchovies love you and your plastic strip of nametag,
your rumpled apron and mock-turtle hairband.
How the silvered light becomes you at three a.m.

How your carbonated cheer infects the products
passing through your ringed, svelte fingers.
And how you sigh as we write our checks
or proffer cash or slide Optima between the slots.
Oh, endless, flapping receipts trailing like festoons!

Amy, life is good. Careful, Doyle, with the light bulbs.
We need every glowing filament. Our houses are dark.
And don't dream of kissing Amy in the stock room.
Her splendid boyfriend waits in a purring Sunbird
in the cold, windy night, the snow falling just right.
Besides, you're too abnormal, son. For a girl like Amy.
Who touches our money and everything we buy,
who weighs the potatoes, gives change and drags out
that meaty *thaaank yieu* so sweetly we want to die.

The Night We Cut the Pineapple

1.

For three days it waited on the kitchen counter
propped on lotus feet like a sturdy, fat Buddha.
Its tough skin bulged with mandalas.
The long ripening candied each room
with wafts of sugar and tropical ease
that defeated the gloom of this mountainous ice,
the darkness, locked doors, and snow.
Here Spring strains forward, halts,
reverses itself, surges again, toys with our hope.
So I declared the fruit, direct from Oahu
according to its tag, a symbol of deliverance,
and promised the impatient children that soon,
soon we would cut it open.

2.

I'm from the deep south (the briny Gulf lapping
at our toes) where we don't need redemption,
but my two little girls, two and four,
know only winters that drag the spirit
into dark sloughs; scrambling out of doors
is reserved for a strict quarter of the year
when skeletal, bleak boughs craving relief,
erupt into life (but wither again as the eye blinks).
No lusty banana trees here, no eternal, lacey ferns,
no colors!–no creamy poinsettia in December,
crepe myrtle exploding year-round, figs gushing
in their sockets on branches slick with lichen,
no sweet olive or soapy four o'clocks

or velvety chameleons panting for breath,
mosquito hawks swooping above lagoons.
The sun itself is so rare we tend to forget it.
I want for my daughters the scherzo of heat,
their foreheads awash in sweat, midnights so balmy
they can dance naked under the moon like savages.

3.

So I taunted them with the pineapple—
"Any time now, girls," I promised, "any time"—
and it became our icon of tangible joy.
On Saturday night, like a solemn, officious priest,
I steered them into the kitchen and presided
from the counter. Their faces squirmed with gladness.
"Do you know what time it is, monkeys?" I asked.
The older, Claire, could not contain herself, gyrated
in her bones. "Time to cut the pineapple!" she cried.
And both began to dance and hoot and squeal.
"The pineapple! The pineapple!" they screeched.
The rafters seemed to sway, the windows buzzed.

I withdrew our longest, sharpest knife from a drawer
and carried it, along with bowls, to the table.
The monkeys, so tiny in normal chairs,
fretted over the knife as they wiggled by my side.
I clutched the dense fruit with both hands,
inhaled its surface and held it under their noses.
They smelled with closed eyes and giggled.
With a single, graceful swoop, I sliced off the top.

Oh the blast of pure Hawaiian joy, the scent
of light and frothy ocean suds, honking seagulls!

We piled the slices into three bowls.
I cut tiny thumbnails for the baby, strips for Claire,
then attacked an entire wedge with my teeth.
It was so good we could not speak; it was juicier than juice;
it tasted like every fruit we could name—bananas,
mangos, cherries, watermelon, guavas, pears—,
our tongues seized with the primal tang of magic.
"Girls," I finally sighed, "we're in paradise."
"What's paradise?" Claire asked. "More?" from Maddie.
I cut new thumbnails and geometric strips,
dabbed their fingers with a wet paper towel,
wiped residue from my beard and the knife.
"Remember this night we cut the pineapple,"
dreamily and joy-choked, I cried.

IV.

Dirges

The Lord of Misrule

I'm six or seven, and we're standing
on Canal Street, my dad, mom, and sister,
who's too young to remember any of this.
It's late February but so hot
the air ripples like cellophane.
The sky, a scratched sheet of slate,
dangles over Maison Blanche; the crowds
between us and storefront glass
threaten to stampede at any moment.
But you never give up a place
on the front row, not for your life.
Rex has already passed, and now
the usual make-shift krewes out of Gretna
and Algiers in ancient, beat-up trucks
decorated with festoons, crepe paper, and glitter.
The stink of moldy hay and stale beer
mesh with horse droppings in the street
and motorcycle fumes.
But it's good to be here.
Masses of screaming, happy people
scurrying for worthless largesse.
My sister and I have already caught
more beads and doubloons than we need,
but that's the idea—amassing doodads
and trinkets out of pure greed
because it's Mardi Gras
and that's what you do.

A primed pick-up lurches before us
only to sputter, cough, and stop.
It looks like any other parade truck
but it's idling, so we notice the theme:
Acadian Paradise.

A loudspeaker blasts bluegrass
and the people aboard cavort
to the beat like mimes.
The whole procession has come to a halt.
We hate when this happens
because after a while the krewe
stops throwing and everyone gets bored.
This one young guy is so drunk he hangs
over a rickety wooden rail of the truck.
His hair is slicked back with pomade
and his face, smeared with white paint.
In one hand he clutches a bottle of Dixie,
in the other, a Zulu coconut.
He's having a great time, laughing,
flirting with pretty girls in the crowd,
puking onto the asphalt, handing out
entire plastic bags of glass beads
strung in Czechoslovakia.
We like him because he's not stingy.
He leans way over, nearly upside down,
to give my sister one of those bags.
A band starts up in the distance,
snare drums, trumpets, Sousa,
and the parade rolls again.

Acadian Paradise backfires, lunges,
and the young guy topples over the rail,
his head pinned under a rear tire.
It happens instantaneously
and the crowd's roar abruptly stops.
The silence feels like pressure
at the bottom of the sea.

Nothing moves except the black,
vulcanized, dusty, rimless, splotched tire
which takes forever to crush his skull.
We hear a rip, the way it sounds when
you tear off the outer shell of a coconut.
Someone cries out. The truck screeches
to another halt. We see the mangled head,
bloody now with yellowish fluid
seeping out of what were once ears.
How could we not? We're on the front line,
dad, mom, my sister and I, my white
and brown shoes are maybe three feet
from the damage. And they're wet.
The young man's body quivers
and then fuses for good with the street.
The crowds remain eerily silent.
The driver kneels down and howls.

I start to scream and jump up and down.
Just jump, that's what I do and scream.
Mom takes one hand, Dad the other,
and they push me and my sister
through a turbulent sea of bodies.
We're blocks away, and I'm still hysterical.
Dad finally cradles me in his arms
and carries me to the Dodge wagon
parked on Elysian Fields,
a long walk from Canal Street.
They throw my shoes out of the window
as we race home—
and my sister's bag of foreign beads too.
Sometimes I think our flight
from that obese Tuesday has never really ended,

that my scream lies buried in a street sewer
like some one-of-a-kind carnival bauble.
And I remember him, the generous, jovial young man,
his face white as Florida, who tossed us a life.

Photographs

I'm thumbing through a volume
called *Great Photographers*
and come across an early portrait
of Charles Baudelaire by
Etienne Carjat.
His eyes are fleurs but not *du mal;*
rather, his eyes have seen pain,
grief, devastation, the ills of the world.
Flowers of brooding and ruin.

I had stored the book in my attic
decades ago and forgot about it
until now. Between the pages
I find one of my own photographs,
probably when I used the Leica
I inherited from Dad.
It's a woman kneeling on the sand
of some beach, probably Florida,
probably Destin, where I once romped.
Hard to identify her because her back
faces the camera and it's difficult
to discern the color of her hair.
So I don't remember who she is
but assume it's someone I knew well
back then.

I hate photographs because they define
the limits of our imagination;
I love them because they memorialize
the split seconds of our existence.

And here again is Baudelaire, *mon frère,*
knowing full well that someday, someone
will stare at his rough-hewn face
and he will not be around to sanction
or witness the witnessing.
And the woman—she faces the sea.

Death Is . . .

    a nursery rhyme

. . . hairline in the rib; the vein's thistle;
flaking lacquer of the skull; rivet in the brain;
rotten tooth; supreme, gregarious Other;
bruised magnolia leaf; Great Mother;
final quark and blackest hole; D-minor;
nirvana; punk on a street corner;
    birds tacked on the skeletal, wintry tree;
a neighbor's cough; sine qua non;
charred wick; spiders in the groin;
possum stiff in a ditch; Sargon the Great;
the smirking non-thing-in-itself; too late;
one divided by none; an error, Sir;
the blur in your bloodless, blind mirror.

About the Author

Two volumes of Louis Gallo's poetry, *Crash* and *Clearing the Attic*, will be published by Adelaide in the near future. His work has appeared or will shortly appear in *Wide Awake in the Pelican State* (LSU anthology), *Southern Literary Review, Fiction Fix, Glimmer Train, Hollins Critic, Rattle, Southern Quarterly, Litro, New Orleans Review, Xavier Review, Glass: A Journal of Poetry, Missouri Review, Mississippi Review, Texas Review, Baltimore Review, Pennsylvania Literary Journal, The Ledge, storySouth, Houston Literary Review, Tampa Review, Raving Dove, The Journal (Ohio), Greensboro Review*, and many others. Chapbooks include *The Truth Change, The Abomination of Fascination, Status Updates and The Ten Most Important Questions*. He is the founding editor of the now-defunct journals, *The Barataria Review,* and *Books: A New Orleans Review.* He teaches at Radford University in Radford, Virginia.